How to be a Lady

Zymurgy Publishing 2005

A CIP catalogue record for this book is available from the British library.

Cover design Nick Ridley

Printed in the UK by
CPI William Clowes Beccles NR34 7TL
ISBN 978 1 903506 19 6

Published by Zymurgy Publishing,
Newcastle upon Tyne

10 9 8 7 6 5 4 3

For my girlfriends and especially my mum. With thanks, love, flowers and sometimes chocolate (although not for Cath as she prefers goat's cheese).

If being a lady in its traditional sense doesn't mean anything to you and you are unable to relate then this book is for you. It's an ideas book of possible ways to navigate a modern world independently. It's more aubergine than pink; the antithesis of the powder-puff.

This book is for those who:

– are the first on the dance floor and the last to leave a party
– have that extra piece of cake
– blow their wages on an item of clothing
– are not too dignified for the dodgems
– like to drink beer and champagne
– eat sun-dried tomatoes and brown sauce (but not at the same time)
– laugh in the face of: low carb, fat free, half caff . . .

Stand By Your Beds

It's not called a regime for nothing but think more *Dad's Army* rather than *Bad Lads Army*.

A lady's 'beauty' regime (meaning taking care of those spots and not the conventional consumerist 'how to spend all your dough trying to look like Kate Moss knowing you'll never get there') is easy but infused with ritual.

Face Time

A lady's most powerful communication tool is not her mobile phone but her face. The Top 3 beauty procedures should therefore be: taking her make-up off at the end of every day, possessing a decent moisturiser and drinking lots of water.

Home Alone

Doing a home face-pack once a fortnight can only improve face matters. To augment the formalities a lady should look to one or two sources of products in order to take advantage of increasingly common loyalty schemes. These include discounts and freebie products and treatments.

Home Alone 2

Macaulay Culkin did it and look where he is now. The point is doing home treatments as often as possible. You can pamper and save money at the same time. If this sounds boring to you start by trying to watch *Coronation Street* with no make-up on.

Steam Room

Pretend you've got a cold and hold your face over a bowl of boiling water for 10 minutes in your bedroom once a fortnight. It's cheaper than belonging to a gym, but for a totally authentic experience acquire a foot infection if possible.

Wax On, Wax Off

Karate *Kid* fans - welcome. Home waxing is only for the brave and/or skint. Wholly gratifying if done well and completely as you get to see your removed hairs up close. It can be terrifying if your mirror is angled awkwardly.

Salon Savvy

For professional bikini topiary a beauty salon is the only way to go. Creative downstairs hairs are fun in the right hands. For legal reasons a professional bikini wax is highly recommended before a beach holiday - trapping small children in your overgrown hair can lead to litigation.

"Expect nothing. Live frugally on surprise."

(Alice Walker)

Don't fly to extremes, live there. As independent ladies we can have our shoes and wear them. There is a strong case for financial planning in these economic times so ladies of moderate means can have it all (well, most of it). The trick is to prioritise and compromise. For example, if you love shoes buy them - but take a packed lunch to work for a week.

Car Insurance for Ladies

Ladies almost always pay less for their car insurance, so seek out a broker or website and save. It is worth checking before you renew.

Clearly ladies are safer drivers and presumably insurers aren't even bothered if we drive in heels or espadrilles.

Emergency Supplies

Keep an 'emergency £2' in your handbag at all times and forget about it. The amount does, of course, depend on which part of the country you live in. Just remember it's there for when you need it. It's like having £100 in a Post Office account that your grandparents set up in the 1970s.

"The only guy a girl can depend on is her daddy."

(Frenchy in *Grease*)

A lady should have a man:

Who spoils her
Who supports her endeavours
Who makes her feel sexy
Who challenges her intellectually
Who complements her life

Most importantly - it is imperative that these men never know about or get to meet each other.

Digging The Scene

Single ladies are more equipped than ever to play the dating 'game' (that's all it is after all). We know what we want, we have our own money and we have the power of reason. We don't need a man other than for pleasure. So, to borrow from *Pretty Woman*, "we say who, we say when, we say how much."

Game On

The game starts during our teens. It's like playing *KerPlunk* - you take out a few sticks (literally and figuratively) then the balls drop. Thereafter it becomes interesting and a lady must play the game on her own terms. Above all a lady should remember a boyfriend doesn't have to be for life, he can be just for Christmas.

Commitment Phobia

It's not only blokes who can't spell commitment (one t). If you can't even commit to a microwave meal there's no need to panic. Ladies like to play the field, choose their own music, enjoy their own friends - whatever. There's no excuse for settling, if your heart's not in it, just for the sake of it.

Making the First Move

No longer just for the men, ladies are prone to making the first move more than ever - and why not? Hooray for equality. Men are hugely flattered by ladies who come-on to them especially if they believe it was all their own idea in the first place.

Conversation

Whether on a date or not, knowing a little bit about a range of subjects is generally better than specialising in a single topic. This keeps a lady's partner in dialogue interested and a lady interesting. So keeping conversation light and generalist is a good way to keep it going and sussing out if it's worth taking any further.

No Tears Before Bedtime

Some 'girls' (you know who you are) use waterworks to get what they want. Ladies, however, know that this betrays their gender and it is a weak-minded sister who employs this tactic in life.

Cabbage is Not the Only Soup

One way to gauge a man's intentions. What is his favourite soup?

<u>Soup Flavour</u> . . . .

Instant or Cup a Soup . . . .

Soup of the Day . . . .
Home—made . . . .
Lentil . . . .
Tomato . . . .
Mulligatawny . . . .
Mushroom . . . .

Chicken . . . .
Nettle . . . .

.. <u>Meaning</u>

.. He just wants instant gratification
   i.e. a one-night stand
.. He's after anything that's on offer
.. He wants to settle down
.. He's impulsive (pulse - geddit)
.. He's down to earth
.. He doesn't know what he wants
.. He's boring unless it's wild
   mushroom
.. He's obviously a hangover casualty
.. He's a Ray Mears outdoor survivalist
   type

Shoe Horn

"If high heels were so wonderful, men would still be wearing them." (Sue Grafton) Here's a fun way to suss out a man's potential - compare him to shoes:

Flip-Flops
Purely for the summer (a May to September affair)
Stilettos
They're gorgeous, flashy party goers that you can only stand for a short period
Espadrilles
Hippy, vegetarian, they like long walks on the beach

Trainers/Pumps
Go anywhere, do anything, practical and comfortable

Short Heeled Boots
They're classy, trustworthy and give you a bit of a lift

Knee–High Boots
They're sexy, reliable and robust and in it for the long haul as they can be resoled and re-heeled

Shuddering Heights

It's me, I'm Cathy - I've come. A lady knows what she wants in bed, on the stairs, on the sofa... and she tells her guy what 'it' is. It's a massive turn-on for a bloke and she therefore never lets him out of her sight until she gets what she came for.

One-Night Stands

M ae West, bless her, once said "a hard man is good to find" and in the sexual arena ladies have the upper hand (if you like). She can therefore dictate if, when, where and how. Safety is the issue not to compromise on so, in the words of Sgt Esterhaus in *Hill Street Blues*, "let's be careful out there".

Textual Healing

Textual flirting (via mobile phone) is foreplay enhanced by technology. As this is within the boundary of fantasy lying about what you're wearing, doing etc is actively encouraged. Consider this textiquette though - if you move on to picture messaging only go for those body parts above the waist.

Pay as you Come and Go

It's like mobile phones, why commit to a fixed term contract when you can top up when needed? If a lady finds herself embarking on a no strings ongoing sexual adventure the terms need to be discussed beforehand. It's like any other physical transaction. Would you buy electrical goods from Currys without a warranty or a get-out clause?

Can't always get what you want

If a lady can't get what she wants she should at least get what she needs for now from a date/sexual encounter/relationship. Compare, for example, the merits of buying cafetiere over a Gaggia coffee machine.

Aftermath...

Tony, John, Heathcliff, whoever. Men generally are much worse at coping with relationship baggage. We all have baggage but ladies deal with it and move on. This is illustrated at airports - men have less carry on luggage but the bulk of their booty is stashed in the hold for later.

Dump and Dumpee

A strong lady knows that when a relationship has outlived its usefulness, i.e. no longer enhances her life, it's time to get rid. Dumping is empowering once the boxes against keeping a relationship going have all been ticked. If a lady becomes a dumpee then she should bear the situation with dignity and move on.

Sex and Dating Philosophy

If disaster hangs in the air, in any given situation, like yesterday's washing a lady should take comfort from this - not getting what you want can sometimes be an amazing piece of luck.

Say Hello, Wave Goodbye

If a relationship has come to a natural end but neither of you want to start the 'split-up' conversation there are easier ways of parting. Leave a little book of baby names lying around.

Foof Night

A lady needs to get together with her girlfriends on a regular basis. During a 'Foof Night' at home she can reaffirm bonds by catching up with her sewing projects, exchanging beauty tips or sharing shopping anecdotes. Alternatively she can get drunk, slag off blokes and discuss the advantages of the rising oestrogen levels in the water.

Supper/Dinner Party

Supper used to be two rounds of malt loaf during *Prisoner Cell Block H* but it now occurs much earlier and demands more attention and effort. Think not of matching glasses and place-settings, unless you love to cook and organise. Get a take-away instead.

Pubs/Drinking

Avoid pubs/clubs which have bulldog type security - they're rough. The only time bouncers work in your favour is on the door of a gay bar to check that you're not on the pull. Alternatively go to real ale pubs which are non-threatening environments - have you ever seen a puffa jacket down the *Coach and Horses*?

Getting a Round In

Ladies are just as likely as blokes to be at the bar these days. We generally precede them at the bar as well - getting the first round in earns us a sit down for at least an hour.

"Every time
I close the
door on reality
it comes in
through the
windows."

(Jennifer Unlimited)

Superwoman

We'd all love to be superwomen but the reality is we are only human. Self-preserve by doing what you can do today and leaving what you can't until tomorrow - it will still be there.

One Bit or Two Love?

Lavatorial attendants have come a long way from handing out toilet paper and going around with the mop. They now occupy a variety of establishments and offer a cornucopia of confections, some of which you can even eat. So a lady needs the appropriate coinage for these trips to avoid having to change a fiver from the tip tray.

Fight!

Haven't we always adored being fought over by dishy blokes in tight trousers with a crowd of onlookers, er, looking on? Abso-bloody-lutely. As a lady though the trick is to maintain a distant nonchalance until the hurly-burly's done, when the battle's lost and won, and not to give them the money to release the supermarket trolleys.

There's Somebody at the Door

Keep your full length dressing-gown handy and your path clear because if the doorbell goes (it could be the postman on a dawn raid or your neighbour wanting to borrow a ladder) you don't want to be answering it in your pants and vest.

Building Sites

If you are unfortunate enough (depends entirely on the way you look at it) to encounter a building site take this with you. Don't walk past with your head down pretending it's not happening if you get wolf-whistled. Engage them in conversation and you will either never have to deal with their ogling again or you will end up dating the hunkiest man on site.

Farting in Bed (FIBing)

If you're a FIBer be proud of it (naturally this includes going undercover to enjoy the olfactory part as well). You can of course FIB contentedly if you are alone but a lady needs to assess the FIBing policy of any partner before letting rip through the pocket-sprung mattress.

More Front than Brighton Beach

If your colleagues (usually male) are suddenly very interested in hovering over you and you haven't just opened a packet of chocolate digestives consider that they may be trying to get an eyeful of your cleavage. If you suss them, announce that it is in fact *National Cleavage Week* and that staring is encouraged. Game over.

Playing Away

If you remember Brian Cant you've probably had to deal with this one. Your mate's boyfriend has been spotted out with a lady who isn't your mate. Tactics? Pretend to 'bump' into him and face him out.

Trip 'Em Up and Start Again

If you are a wheely case type of gal there is a strong possibility that you may trip somebody up one day as you glide way out in front of your hair straighteners and spare undies. If this happens don't get drawn into a conversation with the tripee who throws his/her arms aloft in disgrace. Simply apologise and stroll on.

Tripee Long Stocking

I f you become a tripee of the wheely case type don't fall into the arm flailing, scene stealing trap. Desist, be cool, demand an apology and respectfully move on.

Voting Rights (and Wrongs)

Ahh Suffrage. Women tied themselves to railings and even lost their lives so ladies could have the right to vote. It may seem like a pointless exercise but exercise is good for us as we know. As it is now our right to be part of the 'democratic' process we should use it, without trying to chat-up the exit pollsters.

Relax, Don't Do It

Try not to sing along to your mobile radio, Walkman or iPod on public transport. You may genuinely believe you're Chaka Khan or Beyoncé after a double espresso but no one wants to hear it. Mouth the words behind a paper if you must and get into it there instead.

Meeting the Outlaws

A lady needs to be herself at all times and if she's meeting the in-laws a little of why she's managed to get their son off the streets goes down well. Topics to stay away from though should include her previous relationships, any visits to the clap clinic (however hilarious) and Ferrero Rocher.

"Civility costs nothing and buys everything."

(Lady Mary Wortley Montagu)

Complain with Class

Think about this when you need to make a complaint. You set high standards for yourself and you should expect the same from retailers. Meet them halfway by being positive to get their attention, then outline what you're looking for as an outcome.

Nipple Therapy

I f you've been on your feet and they're giving you what for take advantage of any waiting time at pelican crossings. The tactile paving (nipples sticking out of the ground that show visually impaired people where they are) at the crossings can be used to massage angry feet.

"Whenever I prepare
for a journey I prepare
as though for death.
Should I never return,
all is in order."

(Katherine Mansfield)

Hide and Seek

Should a situation arise, by telling your closest girlfriend beforehand where your sex toys are hidden, she can search for and destroy the evidence before the police, Inland Revenue and your mum and dad arrive.

"When a woman is badly dressed, you notice the clothes. When a woman is well dressed, you notice the woman."

(Coco Chanel)

Work

It entirely depends on what you do for a living of course. If you have to wear a uniform celebrate. Oh yes, there are no dilemmas in the mornings if your work outfit has already been chosen for you (think grass is greener). A general rule to workplace dress if you have the choice - no boobs please we're British.

Rest

If you're home alone anything goes. The fantasy is that you recline in your faux fur trimmed negligé to watch *Sex and the City*, the reality is you love your waffle dressing-gown accompanied by a *Walnut Whip*. In bed you can delight in an egg-custard tart wearing your grandad's pyjamas and no one will know.

Play

If a lady is out of her teens then her boob tube needs to be handed down. Skirts, however short, are acceptable at any age with the addition of tights or stockings as the years roll on. Knee-high boots are fab to accessorise with for a spot of social experimentation.

Rock 'n' Don't Roll

For formal evenings the pinnacle of etiquette, *Debrett's*, advises "strapless and very precarious boned dresses are best avoided, as it is not unknown . . . for the wearer to launch herself in one direction and the dress to move resolutely in the other." It is acceptable to "expose a generous amount of decolletage." If you have to go all girlie, and it is a party, they further advise doing "gentle gymnastics and a certain amount of jumping about to test the safety factor" of the dress

before leaving the changing room. That way you won't please "lecherous old buffers".

Wardrobe Staples

A lady needs some classic pieces in her wardrobe (dress, jacket, trousers, overcoat) that are tailored and of the highest quality she can afford. The cost of these garments will be forgotten long before their real worth is appreciated.

Urbane Outfits

A lady must be prepared for anything and therefore so must her wardrobe. She must at least have, at a moment's notice, a kick-ass outfit to get her through an interview and a blow-his-mind seductive number to get her through a date.

The Little Black Dress

Oh and the Little Black Dress (LBD). It has been proclaimed as a must–have in any lady's wardrobe for decades and still not enough has been said about it. The LBD is slimming, goes with everything and most importantly you can spill things on it and it still comes back for more.

Knickers

Ladies have two types of knickers — black ones the size of an atom or white ones the size of Buckinghamshire (Jo Brand). When a lady is going out she should be ready for any occurrence: animal, vegetable or genital. The best advice is therefore to accessorise knicker-wise the best your smalls drawer can manage.

Staying Over

All you really need is a t-shirt that covers your vag (every lady has one) and a hair scrunchie if you've anything longer than a crew cut (to avoid a hair don't). Your hostess should provide everything else. If you're staying over with a man the scrunchie is all that is required (grrr).

Pants People

Is there a rule as to when/if to pack a spare pair of knickers if you're staying overnight with a man? If a lady is being spontaneous then no spare knickers are required. If the event is premeditated then she will need spare knickers, toothbrush, cleanser and moisturiser, some exfoliating equipment... sod it, it's getting cumbersome.

Lord (or Lady) of the G-String

Builder's Bum isn't attractive on a builder. G-strings have become the antithesis of what they were designed to achieve - concealing a Visible Panty Line (VPL). A bizarre trend has seen g-strings PROMOTING VPL which is neither understood or desirable. The cheese grater effect - non merci.

Tummy Trouble?

If you go to your doctor with a stomach problem and (s)he says "Yes, it's bloody enormous" (Jo Brand again) tummy control pants can assist. Trinny and Susannah swear by them, and they can be handy for a big night out, but the fat's gotta go somewhere. They have also been known to suffer *coitus interruptus* on the wearer - they're tough to get off.

Driving Shoes

Boring - yes, sensible - yes, necessary - triple yes. Walk to your car in your favourite Jimmy Choo's or Clarks but swap 'em for a pair of driving shoes once you're in. Your feet will love you for it and nobody will know that you've got a ten year old pair of Primark flats with the back hanging off under the pedals.

Push Bike

Nerys Hughes in *The District Nurse? Dim Diolch!* Street aware ladies buy their bikes to last - in a man's style which has a high crossbar, is higher spec and more robust than a lady's bike. No basket up front required, the only modification needed is a comfy wide gelled saddle. Panniers - yes, saddlebags - who, me?

Bus/Train

For a truly modern independent experience try using public transport once in a while. For added interest recreate the last round of *Crackerjack* - pile up on shopping (cabbages optional) and try to juggle your ticket/travelcard at the same time.

Car

Leave behind the 'ladies must keep their knees together when entering and exiting their boyfriend's sports car' in the wake of your turbo engine. Ladies have their own sports cars now and they can enter and exit how they bl**dy well feel like.

Aeroplane

Smart ladies hold all their essentials in a carry on case. A vanity case is great for all out glam. Tweezers though are forbidden and will be confiscated at check-in if found. Substitute with condoms because, should the opportunity arise, a lady doesn't want to find herself in the wrong kind of mile high club.

Come fly off the handle with me

When abroad it is a given that we should know how to navigate the local language by way of: "hello", "please", "thank you" and "can I have two beers please?" A favourable outcome is never obtained by shouting louder in English and using semaphore.

Born to Bum

When airlines overbook in Economy class some lucky passengers get bumped up to Business. Ladies who achieve this look businesslike and as if they were born to it. Be aware that this doesn't work on charter flights to Alicante.

"What is this life if,
full of care,
We have no time to
stand and stare?"

from the poem *Leisure* by W H Davies

Cinema

Gentlemen's Films

Seven Brides for Seven Brothers. . . . .
Flash Gordon . . . .
The Dirty Dozen . . . .
The Shining . . . .
Dirty Harry . . . .
Butch Cassidy & the Sundance Kid. . . .
The Pianist. . . . .
Gladiator. . . . .
The Deer Hunter . . . .
Carry on Camping. . . . .

Ladies' Films

- Four Weddings and a Funeral
- Flashdance
- Dirty Dancing
- Shine
- When Harry Met Sally
- Thelma and Louise
- The Piano
- Pride and Prejudice
- Good Will Hunting
- Carry on Doctor

Television

<u>Gentlemen's TV</u>

Starsky & Hutch . . . .

Top Gear. . . . .

The Bill. . . . .

Quincy. . . . .

Men Behaving Badly . . . .

Judge Jugs . . . .

Spooks. . . . .

The Sweeney. . . . .

I Claudius . . . .

Columbo. . . . .

Ladies' TV

. . Cagney & Lacey

. . What Not to Wear

. . Casualty

. . Dr Quinn Medicine Woman

. . Sex and the City

. . Judge Judy

. . Prime Suspect

. . Minder

. . I Dream of Genie

. . Murder She Wrote

"And as for some happy ending, I'd rather stay single and thin."

(*Mulder and Scully* Catatonia)

Treadmill/Crosstrainer

Universally and incontrovertibly the ONLY place for a lady to mount either of the above machines is directly under an air-conditioning outlet. This way she can maintain a glow rather than a sweaty heap and expel air i.e. fart without offence.

Jacuzzi

A lady can easily derive an obscene amount of pleasure (and not let on) in a jacuzzi even with her swimmers on by locating an air outlet and sitting on it.

Sauna/Turkish Bath

Gorillas in the mist (and gorillas in our midst if it's a mixed session). Go for gold with this one as the whole point is to sweat a dozen cobs a minute. There is no way a lady can maintain her dignity under such conditions so ladle on the water and laugh.

Rowing/Cycling Machines

This equipment is generally placed right at the foot of the TV screens so a lady is forced to choose her viewing along with the resistance settings (it's good time management). So plug in and play but before you start make sure it's not a specially extended *Location, Location, Location*.

Quickie Cardio

Going to the gym doesn't sound like a perfect start to a lady's big night out but it so is especially if she's going out after work. A quick cardio workout peps you up after a long day, for that all over glow for later, plus you can use the gym's facilities to shower and change afterwards.

Handbags and the Snot Rags

Make-up bag
mobile phone
travelcard (public transport users)
purse containing cards and money
keys
tissues/wipes
emergency tampon (rotate every two years to avoid non-toxic shock at finding it neglected with bits of chewing gum and cigarette packet foil stuck to it)

Facts of Life

It's amazing any of us ladies turn out balanced at all. As we grow up our mothers tell us we represent the family every time we leave the house and our fathers refuse to kiss us whenever we wear lippy. The issue is we never know when we're likely to bump into a potential suitor.

Shoes

"Give a girl the correct footwear and she can conquer the world."

(Bette Midler)

Give her the most gorgeous, fab, can't live without 'em but impractical shoes and she won't make last orders - tottering into the pub after the bell has gone. Think priorities.

Smile

If you can stomach it even if you're not in the mood. If you really can't get the corners of your mouth to curl up and a passer-by yells "cheer up darlin'" tell them politely they know nothing about your situation, then tell them to sod off.

All Style and No Substance

Even if faced with a crisis of confidence, cash or court shoes a lady needs to be well turned out. Self-loathing is OK for indoors watching *Loose Women* but emerging to greet her public she must rise above it. Look like you're winning even if you're not and especially if you don't feel like it.

For fun and entertainment:

Try a sixth or seventh item out in the 5 Items or Less queue at your local supermarket. This is early grounding for when you later blatantly ignore the sign as a pensioner with your mini trolley.

For fun and entertainment:

Hovering just inside the door of a shop (without setting the alarms off if possible) with an item you've picked out at random is the best way to get a shop assistant's attention if you require anything.

For fun and entertainment:

If a lady has a favourite item of clothing she needs at least one spare. Use the erratic stock levels to mess with the security guards' heads and visit the same shop every day for a week looking for said item. The hunter soon becomes the hunted.

Bra Fitting

The value of undergarments should never be underestimated. They make us feel good underneath and our clothes fit better. Lingerie departments with a bra fitting service should be sought out and utilised. Hitlers with measuring tapes they may be (they always have at least two) but investments can go down as well as up.

Personal Services

Don't think Julie Walters in rubber but department store personal shoppers. They're free (for everyone) and save you from wading through piles of, however well presented, stuff. We all know that when we're looking for something specific we can never find it anyway.

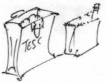

And All Because...

The lady doesn't love petrol station purchased *Milk Tray* anymore being ski delivered by a stereotypically mysterious *Bond* type through the snow. A lady buys her own organic *Green & Black's* that doesn't give her spots.

Beauty Counter Face-Off

Department store beauty counters are scary places and the sales assistants that patrol them terrifying. So don't take make-up advice from bright pink lippy wearing, blue eyebrowed, satsuma faced 'beauty consultants' - it's not clever and it's not fashion.

The Me Ring

This is a growing trend among modern ladies who won't/can't wait for a man to buy a ring for them. It's empowering for a lady to buy a bit of bling to tell her how much she means to herself and how she admires her choice. It is an industry created phenomenon but who cares?

The One

Having one special piece of jewellery that you wear every day says more about you than boxes and bags of stuff collected over the years. It could be a second-hand piece of plastic as long as it means something to you.

Cars

Males and females look for different things when buying a car:

Male

Rear spoiler . . . .
State of the art CD/MP3 player . . . . .
Pull down sun shield . . . .
Heated rear window . . . .
Tough car mats . . . .
Performance . . . .
Smell . . . .
Functionality . . . .
0-60 speed . . . .

<u>Female</u>

. . . A spacious parcel shelf
. . . Cup holder
. . . Pull down vanity mirror (with lights)
. . . Heated front seats
. . . Soft mats (to avoid scuffing heels)
. . . Colour
. . . Shape
. . . Reliability
. . . Miles per gallon

Emailing Your CV

Choose your most vanilla flavoured email account for this purpose or even create a new ID from a range of free online account providers. A lady doesn't want a prospective employer responding to partygirl@hotmail.com

Interviews

The traditional etiquette manuals for ladies didn't include techniques to employ at interview because ladies just did lunch. Now ladies also have jobs - yay. When asked what your weaknesses are don't start with "chocolate".

Rejection

Is a dish best eaten lukewarm. Every time your application for employment is unsuccessful, and you get knocked-back, consider it a positive thing. It may be an old wife's tale (she's actually middle-aged) but for every ninth "no" you get a "yes". So celebrate the negatives.

"Ambition bites the nails of success" (The Fly U2)

Ladies can become legends in their own lunchtimes by having sweets on their desks to attract and trap interesting people. Equally, biscuits can get you on the road to Damascus.

Don't Thank Me

Reputations can be lost in the fall of a paperclip so don't tell your boss if (s)he's particularly well co-ordinated one day that they wouldn't look out of place in IKEA!

Computer Bug

If you're addicted to email and the Internet you're not alone. Be alert to office spies though if you're checking personal messages and be deft with the minimise button. Plus, bring an IT support worker into your circle so they can assist in a crisis and let you know which level of monitoring software they are installing.

Rush Half–Hour

If you're a lady who can't do breakfast before work, even though you know it's a great foundation to the day, obstruct the long wait till lunch by getting a coffee on the way. Nab a few extra napkins while you're at it to keep the handbag tissue tally healthy.

Shorthand

Shorthand is enjoying a renaissance thanks to the iPod generation. Being able to use shorthand is as relevant now as when ladies were first asked to 'take a letter' but now in a different way. It's a whole new language for the too busy to spell properly - lng lv th nu Esperanto.

Txt/Email Shorthand Guide

For mobile phone and email communicators shorthand is even shorter:

x - kiss

o - hug

lol - lots of love/laugh out loud

:-[- I have a square jaw

:-p - I've got a dodgy lip

q:) - I'm a baseball cap wearer

;)8x - I've got big boobs AND I'm cheeky

On-Street

When accosted on the street by a brightly dressed, clipboard–wielding, smiling marketer try responding with:

"I'm not in the habit of giving my bank details to strangers."

"I already contribute to Oxfam/Save the Children/Amnesty International."

"I went paintballing last month, would you like to see my bruises?"

Junk Mail

Do return mail NO LONGER AT THIS ADDRESS and register your details with the *Mail Preference Service*." MPS online allows consumers to register their address via the web to state their wish not to receive unsolicited mail (www.mpsonline.org.uk).

Telephone

There is no need to get into a political debate about the location of the call centre, simply state "I have registered my details with the *Telephone Preference Service*." TPS online allows consumers to register their telephone number via the web to state their wish not to receive unsolicited phone calls (www.mpsonline.org.uk).

Junk Email

Do not reply stating your displeasure at receiving unsolicited email but take advantage of the myriad spam and junk reporting mechanisms within email programs. Register your details with the Direct Marketing Association's *Email Preference Service* (www.dmaconsumers.org/emps.html).

Constipation

If a lady's got some trouble with her bowels we all know that eating greens and bran is the only way to go (if you like), however uninspired we are by this. Laxatives can assist to re-establish a regular pattern and you know they're gonna work because they taste like sh*t.

Smear Tests

Leave your dignity in the reception of the surgery along with the *Good Housekeeping* magazines. If your gynaecologist is a man try not to think about mechanics never owning a car or painting your hallway through the letterbox.

Osteo Aggravation

I f a lady needs therapy or treatment that involves stripping down to her underwear the best advice is to remember to wear some. It could be for a visit to the osteopath or doctor for example. This should avoid the junior school gym class horror of realising that you have to do PE in just your pants.

Ideas for a healthier you:

Try meditation by basically closing your eyes and focussing on breathing. Chanting is optional.

Find your inner child and bring it out to play. Blokes do! This can involve a sandpit if you prefer.

Discover Feng Shui and unblock yourself (not literally). Use, love or dispose of clutter and become a Bagua lady.

Medical Moves

If you have to have some gynaecological treatment and the clinic offers you the opportunity to choose your own music, think it through carefully before making your selection. You may abhore pan pipes, but Abba's greatest hits or other music you might jig along to could get you into trouble.

Bog Off

I f there is a man in your home who always leaves the toilet seat up, in reality there is little chance of training him to leave it down. Be grateful that he lifts the seat up in the first place and leaves it dry for you!

"A man in the house is worth two in the street."
(Mae West)

If a lady has a room to let and some jobs to do around the house she should consider advertising for a housemate that comes with skills as well as the ability to pay rent. Only timeserved tradesmen need apply.

"Loss of virtue in a female is irretrievable; one false step involves her in endless ruin."

(Pride and Prejudice)